You are the apple of God's eye.

Happy Birthday!

Dedicated
to my family and friends...

Michael
Michelle
Gary
Alexis
Jessica
Nancy
Del
Marsha
Jack
Mark
Kathy

Whose fruitful lives
nourish and satisfy my soul!

With a special thank you to Nancy . . .
couldn't have done it without you, my friend!!
And to Mark I am eternally grateful . . .
for your planting this seed in my heart!!

Sweet As Apple Pie

Daily Inspirations for Healthy and Fruitful Living

KARLA DORNACHER

THOMAS NELSON

Copyright 2011 by Karla Dornacher

Published in Nashville, Tennessee by Thomas Nelson. Thomas Nelson
is a registered trademark of Thomas Nelson, Inc.

Unless otherwise indicated, all Scripture quotations are taken from the New
International Version of the Bible (NIV) © 1984 by International Bible Society.
Used by permission of Zondervan Publishing House. All rights reserved.

The New King James Version (NKJV) of the Bible. © 1982,
by Thomas Nelson, Inc. Used by permission. All rights reserved.

The Living Bible (TLB) © 1971. Used by permission of Tyndale House Publishers, Inc.
Wheaton, Illinois 60189. All rights reserved.

The Message (MSG) by Eugene H. Peterson. © 1993. Used by permission of
NavPress Publishing Group. All rights reserved.

The Holy Bible, New Living Translation (NLT) © 1996.
Used by permission of Tyndale House Publishers, Inc., Wheaton, Illinois 60189.
All rights reserved.

New American Standard Bible®. © The Lockman Foundation 1960, 1962, 1963, 1968,
1971, 1972, 1973, 1975, 1977, 1995. Used by permission.

NCV from New Century Version®. © 2005 by Thomas Nelson, Inc.
Used by permission. All rights reserved.

All rights reserved.
No portion of this publication may be reproduced, stored in a retrieval system
or transmitted in any form by any means ~ electronic, mechanical, photocopying,
recording, or any other ~ except for brief quotations in printed reviews, without
the prior written permission of the publisher.

ISBN 978~1~4003~7055~9

Printed in Mexico
11 12 13 14 15 QG 6 5 4 3 2 1

www.thomasnelson.com

Dear Friend,

This book has been such a joy to write and illustrate. Being able to visualize soul~nourishing truths by looking to the common apple reminded me so much of how Jesus taught using objects of nature.

Solomon understood the life~giving properties of the apple when he wrote the proverb, "A word fitly spoken is like apples of gold in settings of silver" (Proverbs 25:11 NKJV). He knew that words, especially God's words, have tremendous power to bring health and healing to our lives.

In this little devotional, I invite you to eat an apple a day of God's golden Word, served in a silver setting of heartwarming, apple~flavored illustrations and stories. As you chew on God's truth and savor the sweetness of it, I pray your heart will be stirred to healthy and fruitful living for God's glory.

In His love,
Karla

Early in the morning I will rise up and seek Thee.

6

🍎 Today's Apple...

Through Jesus, therefore, let us continually offer
to God a sacrifice of praise ~
the fruit of lips that confess his name.
Hebrews 13:15

🍎 Chew on it...

There is no greater fruit, none that is more
pleasing to God the Father, than the fruit of our
praises. To exalt His name, to sing His praises, to
lift our hands and offer up our hearts, is the
ultimate purpose for which we were called. In
those moments when life is a struggle and our
praise is not found in our circumstances, it is
then that our hearts and thoughts are challenged
to focus only on how great God truly is. It is in
those moments that our praise becomes a holy
sacrifice and we remember that all our
fruit~bearing efforts are dependent on Him
and not us . . . and He gets all the glory!

🍎 Savor the Flavor...

Dear Lord, forgive me for using my lips to
grumble and complain when things don't go my
way. You have been so good to me, Lord.
I owe You my life. I owe You my praise.

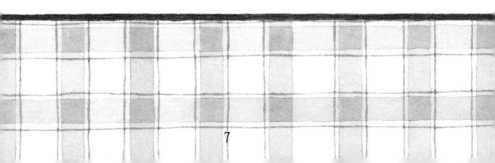

Day 2

🍎 Today's Apple...

A word aptly spoken
is like apples of gold in settings of silver.
Proverbs 25:11

🍎 Chew on it...

Mmmmmmm good! Our words have the power to
nourish and give life or to poison and bring death. God
instructs us to choose life. To speak a word of
encouragement, comfort, or instruction at just the right
moment in time can be as sweet to the soul and as
nourishing to the heart as a gift of golden delicious
apples to both the giver and the receiver. Especially
with sensitive issues, the time and place is as important
as the word itself, so ask God for the wisdom to know
when and where to speak, so the setting will be as perfect
and precious, as the word itself.

😃 Savor the Flavor...

Lord, thank You for creating me as a woman of
influence. Fill my mouth with words that build up and
not tear down. Give me wisdom in the timing as well
as the setting in which I speak, and let my words always
be a blessing to those who hear them.

God desires to speak golden apples
into your life through the precious wisdom of His Word.
Take a few moments to chew on this verse and then describe
the flavor of its sweetness as it feeds your soul.

"I know the plans I have for you," declares the LORD,
"plans to prosper you and not to harm you,
plans to give you hope and a future."
Jeremiah 29:11

Day 3

🍎 Today's Apple...

You did not choose me, but I chose you and appointed you
to go and bear fruit ~ fruit that will last.

John 15:16

🍎 Chew on it...

You were chosen! Isn't that an incredible thought? Out
of all the wild trees of the field, God chose you, lifted
you up out of the brambles and muck, and transplanted
you into His royal orchard! Now, you've always borne
fruit, but before Christ found you, your branches were
spindly and your fruit was fit only for the birds. But
now that the Master Orchardist is overseeing your care,
you're growing in strength and vigor, and your fruit is
holy and fit for eternity.

🍎 Savor the Flavor...

Oh Lord, thank You for choosing me and giving me new
life in Christ. I don't always see holy fruit in my life,
but I do believe You are working in me and through me
to bear fruit worthy of my King.

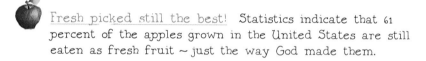
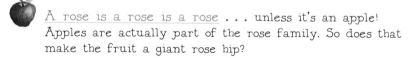
A Bushel Basket of Apple Facts

<u>Fresh picked still the best!</u> Statistics indicate that 61 percent of the apples grown in the United States are still eaten as fresh fruit ~ just the way God made them.

<u>A rose is a rose is a rose</u> . . . unless it's an apple! Apples are actually part of the rose family. So does that make the fruit a giant rose hip?

<u>The apple variety "Delicious"</u> is the most commonly grown in the United States. Delicious by name . . . delicious by taste. Hmmmmmm ~ good!

<u>Have you ever heard of bobbing for oranges?</u> How about for bananas? The reason we bob for apples is because 25 percent of their volume is air, and they'll always rise to the top.

<u>When is an apple really a banana?</u> Okay, never . . . but in early America the apple was called a winter banana, and there's still a variety known by that name today.

Apples 5¢

Early Bird Apple Casserole

This is a wonderfully sweet but nutritious casserole~
Perfect for a ladies brunch or get~together.

Preheat your oven to 350 degrees.

Start by mixing 2 cups of sour cream and ½ cup of brown sugar.
Chill until serving.

Next you want to make your french toast for layering:
12 slices of wheat bread
4 eggs
1 cup half~and~half (or hazelnut creamer)
1 T. butter

Soak bread slices in mixture of whipped eggs and creamer. Preheat
griddle with butter and cook bread on each side until golden brown.

Now you're ready to put it all together . . .
12 thin slices of ham (try the maple~flavored kind!)
2 cups mixed, grated cheddar/jack cheese
1 20~ounce can of apple pie filling   1 cup of granola

In a 9 x 13 baking dish, place 6 slices of the
french toast. Add a layer of all the ham.
Top with 1½ cups of cheese.
Add remaining 6 slices of french toast.
Spread apple pie filling over the top.
Sprinkle with granola.
Bake 25 minutes. Top with remaining
cheese and return to the oven for
5 minutes.

Serve with the chilled sour cream
topping and enjoy!!

14

Day 4

🍎 Today's Apple . . .

We . . . do not cease to pray for you, and to ask . . . that
you may walk worthy of the Lord, fully pleasing Him,
being fruitful in every good work and increasing in the
knowledge of God.

Colossians 1:9~10 (NKJV)

🍎 Chew on it . . .

God has made Himself known to us in nature,
in Scripture, and ultimately in the person of His Son,
Jesus Christ. He wants us to know Him because the
better we know Him, the more we will trust Him. The
more we trust Him, the more we will love Him. The
more we love Him, the more we will want to please Him
and live a life worthy of His love. A life lived for God
will always result in good works ~ good works that will
bear fruit to His glory.

🍎 Savor the Flavor . . .

Father, help me to know You more today than yesterday.
Teach me to hear Your voice and be sensitive to Your
leading so that my life will not be in vain,
but be abundantly fruitful, bringing great pleasure
and glory to You.

 Today's Apple . . .

I praise you because I am fearfully
and wonderfully made; your works are wonderful,
I know that full well.

Psalm 139:14

Chew on it . . .

There are tart apples, sweet apples, crunchy and
juicy apples. There are pie apples, eating apples,
bobbing and drying apples. There are about 2,500
varieties of apples grown in the United States and
about 7,500 worldwide, each distinct enough to be
given its own name. God loves variety and that's
why He created you and me ~ similar in some
ways but very different in others. God made us
each unique individuals so that we would bear
fruit to meet different needs. Don't ever try to be
like me . . . the world needs both of us!

Savor the Flavor . . .

Lord, I praise You for creating me with my own
personality, talents, and strengths. Thank You that
You love me just the way You made me. Help me
to never compare myself to anyone else, but to
use my uniqueness to bear fruit for Your glory.

What makes you different from other women you know? Are you more serious or more playful? Are you more creative or more analytical? Do you like computing more than cooking? List some of the things that make you unique and then ask God to use these qualities to make a difference in your world.

Day 6

🍎 Today's Apple...

God loves a cheerful giver.

2 Corinthians 9:7 (NKJV)

🍎 Chew on it...

I love a good belly laugh. Evidently God does too. In fact,
a paraphrase of these words from the original language
would be: *God delights much in a hilarious giver*. God
wants us to be like Him . . . willing, good~natured, and
joyfully ready to give. Where I live in the Pacific
Northwest, a nine~year~old boy recently asked family
and friends to donate money to a well~known children's
charity rather than give him presents for his birthday.
The amount he raised was extravagant to a nine~year~
old although a drop in the bucket to a large charity.
This story ended up on a local TV station because hearts
are touched by this kind of giving. A hilarious giver is
contagious and a delight to the Lord!

🍎 Savor the Flavor...

Father, thank You for all You have sown into my life.
I am blessed. Show me the seeds I need to sow today.
Help me to be a hilarious, contagious giver,
for in such a person You delight.

Any fool can count
the seeds in an apple.
Only God
can count all the apples
in one seed.

Robert Schuller

Appleberry Tea

This delicious, fragrant tea would be wonderful served
for a luncheon or any large gathering of ladies.

It's easiest to prepare this delightful brew
in a 30~cup coffee maker.

Simply combine the following ingredients and heat:
1 gallon of apple juice
32 raspberry tea bags
16 regular tea bags
1 quart of water
2 teaspoons of lemon juice
½ cup of sugar

Just a tip:
Pour hot water into your teapot as you prepare the tea.
When ready, pour out the hot water and fill with the tea.
This will heat your teapot and keep your tea from
cooling before serving.

For fun: If they're in
season, add a couple of
fresh raspberries to
each cup for a
splash of color!

How sweet are
your words
to my taste,
sweeter than honey
to my mouth!

Psalm 119:103

Day 7

🍎 Today's Apple . . .

A man will be satisfied with good by the fruit of his mouth.
Proverbs 12:14 (NKJV)

🍎 Chew on it . . .

How easy it is for us to fall into a trap of negative
speaking. When we speak badly about others, it's called
gossip. When we speak negatively about ourselves, we
disagree with the truth of whom God says we are in Christ.
When we speak against our circumstances, the Bible calls it
murmuring or complaining. As our ears hear the words we
speak from our own lips, without even realizing it, we are
feeding our own souls with discontent and despair. What
kind of words are you eating? Ask God to help you speak
only those things that are true, honorable, admirable, and
praiseworthy. See if life doesn't start to taste
a little better when you do.

🍎 Savor the Flavor . . .

Father God, help me to be more aware of the words of my
mouth ~ words to myself and to others. Teach me to speak
only words that are in agreement with Your Word
and bring glory to Your Name.

Today's Apple...

Give her of the fruit of her hands,
and let her own works praise her in the gates.

Proverbs 31:31 (NKJV)

Chew on it...

I don't know about you, but I really want my husband to notice
and appreciate when I have worked especially hard for our family.
Whether it is persevering through paperwork, a messy job, or a day
with a sick child, his praise rewards me. And, if he fails to notice,
unlike the Proverbs 31 woman, I just might remind him!

The word *fruit* in Proverbs 31:31 is also translated *reward*.
When a farmer plants an apple seed and diligently takes care of
the seedling, he is eventually *rewarded* with a harvest of apples.
It's the same way for the woman who, with an eternal perspective,
works purposefully to accomplish her daily tasks and nurtures
the life of Jesus in herself and others. Her work will be rewarded
and praised, if not in this life, in the one to come.

Savor the Flavor...

O Lord, help me to be diligent and generous with the work of
my hands. Protect me from the temptation to work for the praises
of others or find my value anywhere else but in You.

 Today's Apple . . .

The seed is the word of God.
Luke 8:11 (NKJV)

 Chew on it . . .

Have you ever thought about how many apples can
grow from a single seed? One seed, one tree . . . but
countless fruit! That's how God's Word is! His Word
has the power to give life ~ and life more abundantly!
From the singular seed of His love, planted into your
heart through the power of His Word, God is able to
transform your life into a tree of great fruitfulness.
You may be only one tree, but your single life has the
incredible potential to impact and influence not only
those closest to you, but generations to come. Are you
letting God's Word transform you today?

Savor the Flavor . . .

Lord, I want a transformed life. Stir my heart to
spend more time with You ~ reading, studying, and
meditating on Your Word, allowing it to mold and
change my life to look more like You.

The fruit of the righteous is a tree of life. Proverbs 11:30

🍎 Today's Apple...

The fruit of the righteous is a tree of life,
and he who wins souls is wise.

Proverbs 11:30 (NKJV)

🍎 Chew on it...

Every day we are given opportunities to offer the
life~giving fruit of God's love to those around us ~ fruit
that has been formed in us, not because of who we are,
but because of who God is in us. God desires this fruit to
be evident in our everyday lives as we reach out and
offer a taste of God's love, acceptance, and forgiveness to
a lost and lonely world through our words and deeds.
This is the fruit that wins hearts to Christ.

🍎 Savor the Flavor...

Lord, help me to remember that every act of love and
kindness is an opportunity to offer Your life~giving fruit
to those who do not know You. Let my branches stretch out
in new ways today.

Dear Father,

Open my eyes
   that I might see,
the opportunities
   You give to me . . .

To be Your hands,
   Your heart, I pray,
and touch all those
   I see today . . .

With words of love
   and affirmation,
to fill their hearts
   with confirmation . . .

That they might know
   Your love is true
and how very special
   they are to You!

Apple Basket Ideas!

Line your basket with excelsior and add a raffia bow. Start with a few juicy apples and then, depending on the occasion, choose a few of the following goodies to finish filling your basket.

A bag of apple chips

Red and green pencils

Sparkling apple cider

Apple erasers

Dried apples in a bag
  or on a string

Caramel apple dip with sticks

Apple cider for mulling with a bag of mulling spices

Apple cinnamon tea

An apple~decorated teacup or mug

Apple~flavored jellybeans

A red and green apple towel

An apple parer

Red and green candles

Apple~shaped cookie cutter

American flags

And, oh yes, don't forget a copy of this little devotional and a note that says, "You are the apple of God's eye!"

🍎 Today's Apple. . .

Give her of the fruit of her hands,
and let her own works praise her in the gates.
Proverbs 31:31 (NKJV)

🍎 Chew on it. . .

Dorcas was a woman who loved God, not just in word but
also with the fruit of her hands. She was known for her
acts of kindness, especially toward the poor. The Bible
tells us that when she died, her friends gathered around
her to mourn their loss. When the apostle Peter arrived to
pray for her, these women, mostly widows, proudly
showed him the robes and other clothing that she had
made for them. No one had to try and make up nice
things to say about this woman ~ her own works brought
her honor and praise. But there's more to the story.
Peter prayed and Dorcas's life was restored! God
apparently had more for her to do.

🍎 Savor the Flavor. . .

Oh Lord, make me more sensitive to the needs of others,
and help me to be more generous with the fruit of my
hands. Protect me, in my giving, from the temptation to
work for the praises of others or to look for my value
anywhere else but in You.

Day 12

Today's Apple. . .

And hope does not disappoint us, because God has poured
out his love into our hearts by the Holy Spirit,
whom he has given us.

Romans 5:5

Chew on it. . .

An apple tree is thirsty for water, knowing that the
amount of moisture it receives will critically affect the
quantity and the quality of its fruit. It sends its roots
down deep into the soil in search of life~giving moisture.
The same can be said of us ~ the greater our desire to
bear fruit that is both eternal and abundant, the thirstier
for God we become. The love of the Lord is a fountain of
living water to our souls, cleansing us from our sin and
giving life to those who drink of it. As we tap into this
never~ending flow of grace through time spent in the
Word and in prayer, there is hope for even the most dry
and stagnant places in our lives to come to life and in
time bear abundant fruit.

Savor the Flavor. . .

Are you thirsty for God's love? Do you long for the water of
His Spirit to fill the dry and stagnant places of your life?
Are you allowing enough time in your day for a thorough
watering of God's Word and soaking it up through prayer?

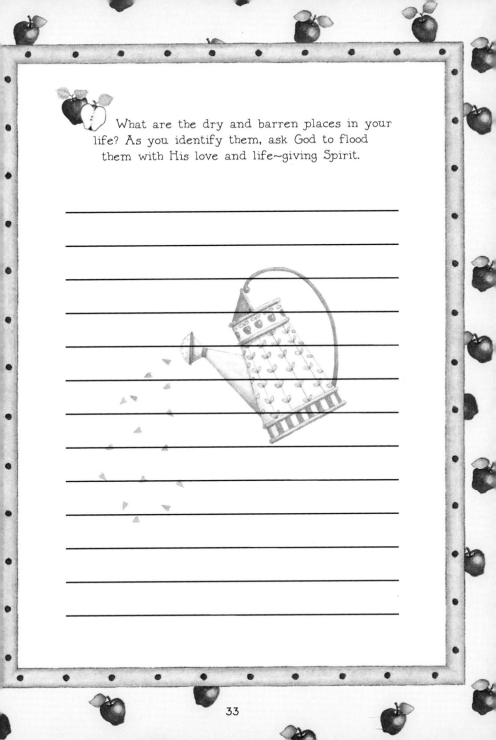

What are the dry and barren places in your life? As you identify them, ask God to flood them with His love and life~giving Spirit.

Day 13

Today's Apple. . .

For two whole years Paul stayed there in his own rented
house and welcomed all who came to see him. Boldly and
without hindrance he preached the kingdom of God and
taught about the Lord Jesus Christ.

Acts 28:30~31

Chew on it. . .

The apostle Paul was under house arrest. His chains
hindered him from moving about freely, but his hospitality
and welcoming heart provided an unhindered place for
others to hear the Word of God. Although his circumstances
seemed rocky, his heart was not. Although imprisoned,
he was fruitful. Paul's "rented house" experience is
particularly meaningful to the woman at home or in
difficult circumstances. It reminds us that whatever season
of life we're in or hindrances we face, we can still make
our homes a place of ministry to *all who enter in*. And it
may even be the most fruitful season of all!

Savor the Flavor. . .

Father, help me to take my eyes off the circumstances that
feel hindering to me and put them back on You. I thank You
for my home. Give me a welcoming heart and the boldness
to share Your love and Your Word with those who enter in.

The LORD bless you and keep you;
the LORD make his face shine upon you
and be gracious to you;
the LORD turn his face toward you
and give you peace.

Numbers 6:24~26

Apple Butter Blessings

Half the blessing of this recipe is that
it starts with using store~bought applesauce!
The rest of the blessing is in its flavor.

2 cups unsweetened applesauce
1½ cups sugar
1 tsp cinnamon
½ tsp allspice
pinch of ginger
pinch of cloves

Combine all above ingredients into a saucepan
and bring to a boil. Reduce heat and simmer
for one hour. Cool and serve.

How easy can it be!

For a tasty treat, mix apple butter with sour cream
for a fruit salad dressing.

Love is a fruit
in season at all times,
and within the reach
of every hand.

♥ Mother Teresa ♥

Day 14

 Today's Apple. . .

You will know them by their fruits.
Matthew 7:16 (NKJV)

 **Chew on it. . .**

Many years ago, we had only one car. I spent my days
alone with my baby and would often yearn for company.
So when a woman knocked at my door and offered to
come visit me every week, I was thrilled. She was
genuinely kind and compassionate and seemed to honestly
care about me as a person. She brought her Bible and we
would study together, but the more I studied on my own,
the more I realized that many of the things she wanted
me to believe did not agree with the Book she gave me to
read. She had an appearance of fruitfulness, but the fruit
of her words did not line up with the truth of Scripture.
How can we know a religious counterfeit? By knowing the
real Jesus and the truth of His Word.

Savor the Flavor. . .

Heavenly Father, I believe that every Word written in
Scripture has been inspired by You and is profitable
in showing me what is true, revealing where I'm wrong,
correcting my mistakes, and teaching me to live for You.
Always remind me to check the fruit I'm being fed by
others, to make sure it's been taken
from Your garden.

Today's Apple. . .

And the seed that fell on the good
ground is like those who hear
God's teaching with good, honest hearts and obey
it and patiently produce good fruit.

Luke 8:15 (NCV)

Chew on it. . .

God is the ultimate seed~sower, and He is forever
seeking fertile heart~soil to plant with the truth and
teachings of His Word. He looks for hearts that are
willing not only to hear Him but also to believe and
obey. Every time we read the Bible or hear a good
sermon, we are giving God the opportunity to plant
the seeds of His truth in our hearts. He knows that
when His Word takes root in our hearts and when
we grow in obedience, fruitfulness is inevitable. And
in due season, if we trust and obey with patience
and perseverance, we will reap the fruit of our faith
and still have plenty to give away!

Savor the Flavor. . .

Heavenly Father, I am so thankful for Your
truth, teachings, and promises. Fill my heart
with Your love so that I will always be open
and yielded to Your Word.

Today's Apple...

No discipline seems pleasant at the time, but painful.
Later on, however, it produces a harvest of righteousness
and peace for those who have been trained by it.

Hebrews 12:11

 Chew on it...

As a young mom I had no idea how to parent. Not
knowing God, I was prone to discipline out of anger and
frustration, not out of love. I am eternally grateful to
the folks who invited me to see a Christian film that
showed me that true discipline flows from a loving heart
and a sincere desire to want the best for the child
because that's how our heavenly Father is with us. When
He sees attitudes and behaviors in our lives that are
harmful to us and keep us from being all that we are
designed to be, He will allow trials and afflictions in our
lives ~ not to harm us but to train us and make us more
fruitful in days to come.

Savor the Flavor...

Heavenly Father, thank You for loving me enough to discipline
me when I need it. Help me to understand that
Your correction is never condemning but is always designed
to bring me closer to You.

🍎 Today's Apple...

This same Good News that came to you is going out all over
the world. It is bearing fruit everywhere by changing lives,
just as it changed your lives from the day you first heard and
understood the truth about God's wonderful grace.

Colossians 1:6 (NLT)

🍎 Chew on it...

I once knew a woman who was headed down a path of
destruction and despair. She kept searching and seeking for
something to make her feel better. She wanted to change but just
didn't know how. I watched her as she read countless self~help
books, tried transcendental meditation, and even followed a cult or
two. But it wasn't until the day she heard the Good News . . . ate
of the fruit of God's amazing grace . . . that her life changed.
A broken life was made whole. An empty heart filled. A wounded
spirit healed. It was a miracle for sure and still is. I know
because this woman was me. What about you? Are you
letting God's Word transform your life?

🍎 Savor the Flavor...

Heavenly Father, give me a hunger for the fruit of
Your Word. Stir my heart to want to spend more time
with You ~ reading, studying, and meditating on Your Word.
Help me to never take Your grace for granted but, instead,
let it change the way I live and love.

There's an angel in my garden,
who watches over me,
I know she smiles as I talk to God
under the apple tree.

Reach for
the highest apple —
you can always
get the lowest ones
later!

Anonymous

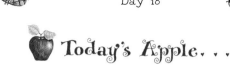

Today's Apple...

Jesus said, "Feed my sheep."
John 21:17

Chew on it...

Before Jesus ascended into heaven, He told one of His followers
to feed His sheep. He wasn't talking about delicious apples from
a tree, nor was He referring to those cuddly, cute lambs of the
field. Jesus was talking about us feeding one another with the
fruit of our lives. We don't have to be preachers or teachers or
scholars to feed others. We don't have to be rich or pretty or
perfect either. We offer spiritual food by giving of ourselves ~
our words, time, talents, and money ~ in the ordinary moments
of our daily lives. That's how we were designed, to bear
fruit ~ fruit that feeds and nourishes Jesus' other sheep.

Savor the Flavor...

Father, help me not to be selfish with the fruit
of my life. It is a privilege to serve You by serving
others. I release my hold on my time, talents, and
resources that together we might feed Your sheep.

Day 19

🍎 Today's Apple...

Those who are planted in the house of the LORD shall
flourish in the courts of our God. They shall still bear fruit
in old age; they shall be fresh and flourishing.

Psalm 92:13~14 (NKJV)

🍎 Chew on it...

I remember the time I arrived at a retreat and discovered
that most of the women present were over sixty~five
years old. As the main speaker that weekend, my heart
sunk as I wondered how my message would be relevant to
their age, to their season of life. As I prayed and asked
God if I should try to alter the message, I heard this little
voice say, "There is no retirement in Christ!" I gave the
message as I had prepared it and it bore fruit. You see,
we can retire from a job, we can even retire as a full~time
parent when our children are grown, but when we've
been planted in the house of our God, we can never
retire from our call and responsibility to bear fruit! And
the promise is, as we continue to bear fruit,
God will keep us fresh and flourishing!

🍎 Savor the Flavor...

Dear Jesus, our culture sometimes devalues those who are
aging in years, but I know You don't. Thank You that we
are able to bear fruit, no matter our age, as we stay
planted in Your presence and plan.

🍎 Today's Apple...

This is to my Father's glory, that you bear much fruit,
showing yourselves to be my disciples.

John 15:8

🍎 Chew on it...

An apple tree naturally produces apples, just as orange
trees bear oranges and we look for peaches on a peach
tree. When people look at us, they want to see the fruit of
Jesus in our lives. God the Father is glorified when our
fruitfulness reveals the nature of His Son. As we allow
the Holy Spirit to freely flow in us and through us, we
will progressively look, sound, and act less and less like us
and more and more like Him. The world is watching,
looking for our fruit, looking for Jesus in the character of
our lives. Who are they seeing when they look at you?

🍎 Savor the Flavor...

Oh Lord, thank You for calling me to follow You and
be Your disciple. You know my heart is for people to see You
through me, so show me, Lord, where I still look too much
like me and not enough like You. Give me
the power to change.

Today's Apple...

He has already tended you by pruning you
back for greater strength and usefulness by
means of the commands I gave you.

John 15:3 (TLB)

Chew on it...

Pruning a plant causes hidden, dormant buds just under the bark
to come to life. Pruning also adds strength to the remaining
branches and prevents the plant from becoming too spread out,
thus affecting its ability to bear high yields of quality fruit. The
same is true for us. Although often painful at the time, we all go
through seasons of fruitful pruning as God removes things from
our lives that hinder our growth. He does this to reveal dormant
areas of our lives just waiting to blossom or branches needing to
be strengthened. In the process, we may become more useful than
we ever dreamed possible because of the experience
of the Lord's pruning in our lives.

Savor the Flavor...

Lord, I desire to grow in strength and usefulness.
Lead me on the path of Your Word in my times
of pruning that my dormant areas might bud
and bear even greater fruit.

Apple of God's Eye Pie

1/2 cup white sugar   1/4 cup firmly packed brown sugar
1/4 cup flour   1 teaspoon of apple pie spice

6 cups peeled, cored, and sliced tart cooking apples
2   9~inch prepared pie crusts, unbaked

1 tablespoon butter   1 teaspoon sugar

Preheat oven to 400 degrees.
Mix together the white sugar, brown sugar, flour, and
apple pie spice in a large mixing bowl.

Add the apples and toss to coat evenly.

Spoon filling into prepared bottom crust.
Drape the top crust over the pie. Fold the edges of the top
crust under bottom crust edge and crimp together with your
fingers to seal it. Cut slits in the top crust to
allow steam to escape.

Brush the top crust with butter and sprinkle with sugar.
Cover edge of crust with 2~inch strips of foil.
Place pie plate on cookie sheet and bake for 35 minutes.
Remove the foil and bake another 10 to 20 minutes
until apples are tender and crust is golden brown.

Cool on rack. Slice, serve, and enjoy!
Taste and see that the Lord is good!

Core Values

Do unto others as you would like them

Respectful
Peaceful
Truthful
Patient
Honest
Kind
Gentle
Joyful
Loving
Helpful
Prayerful
Compassionate

to do unto you.

Luke 6:31

Day 22

 Today's Apple...

He who sows bountifully will also reap bountifully.

2 Corinthians 9:6 (NKJV)

Chew on it...

When I plant my garden, if I only plant a few seeds, I will get only a small crop; but the more I plant, the greater my harvest and my joy. This is a basic principle of life, isn't it? But sometimes we fail to apply this principle to spiritual seed. God has filled the seed packet of your life with His love, His blessing, and His provision in order for you to give it away . . . to scatter His seed through your good works. The more you are willing to give, the more He will supply. Take the seed He's given you, no matter how small it seems to be, and generously sow it into someone else's life with love. Look to God not only to replenish what you've given, but to multiply it back to you so you can sow even more.

Savor the Flavor...

Thank You, Father, for all You have sown into my life . . . I am blessed. Show me the seeds I need to sow today and where to sow them so that others may know how great You are!

 Today's Apple...

May your roots go down deep into the soil of
God's marvelous love.

Ephesians 3:17 (TLB)

Chew on it...

We all need to be valued, and our natural tendency is
to seek out love and affection to meet that need
wherever we can find it. We often move from one
source to another, looking to people and circumstances
instead of to God. The more we are confident in our
position as a child of God, knowing that we have found
an eternal home for our heart in the very love of God,
the less we seek out other sources for approval and
acceptance. The deeper we put down our roots and
become established in His love, the stronger our branches
become to bear His fruit.

Savor the Flavor...

Heavenly Father, forgive me for looking in other places
for the love that only You can give. Help me to dig
deep and experience the fullness of Your love, so that
out of the abundance of my heart I will bear fruit.

Are you seeking your value and sense
of worth in your circumstances or in other
people more than in God? Look up some verses such as
Psalm 139:13~16 or Ephesians 1:3~14 regarding who you are
in Christ and write your thoughts here. Let your roots
go down deeper into His love as you soak up these truths.

Today's Apple. . .

All Scripture is inspired by God and profitable for
teaching, for reproof, for correction, for training in
righteousness; so that the man of God may be
adequate, equipped for every good work.

2 Timothy 3:16~17 (NASB)

Chew on it. . .

We don't always make good food choices, do we?
We want to eat healthy, but each of us, I'm sure, can
think of a few empty calories we consume. Even more
important than what we feed our bodies, however, is how
well we feed our souls. And when it comes to feeding on
God's Word, there are no empty calories. The more we
take in, the more we are nourished; and with every
morsel of instruction and correction we consume, the
healthier we become. Daily dining at God's banqueting
table strengthens our spirits and prepares us for the
good work He has given us to do.

Savor the Flavor. . .

I come to You today, Lord, to feed on Your Scriptures
that I might be adequate and prepared for the work
You have for me. Equip me and then use me I pray.

Jesus answered, 'It is written:
'Man does not live on bread alone,
(*or by apples),
but on every word
that comes
from the mouth of God.'"

Matthew 4:4
(*the apples are mine)

Health Bites

An apple a day keeps the doctor away!
This saying was around a long time
before scientists proved it to be true!

~ Diet~Wise ~
Apples are fat free and average only eighty calories each!

~ Heart~Wise ~
 Apples are cholesterol and sodium free!

~ Digestion~Wise ~
Apples provide dietary fibers that aid digestion!

~ Nutrient~Wise ~
Apples provide 8 percent of the daily vitamin C your body requires!

~ Energy~Wise ~
The easy~to~digest sugars in an apple give the body a boost!

~ Dollar~Wise ~
Apples are plentiful and easy on the pocketbook!

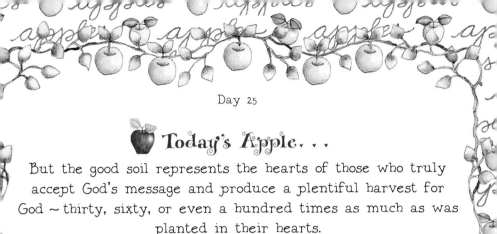

Day 25

🍎 Today's Apple...

But the good soil represents the hearts of those who truly accept God's message and produce a plentiful harvest for God ~ thirty, sixty, or even a hundred times as much as was planted in their hearts.

Mark 4:20 (TLB)

🍏 Chew on it...

God wants to plant the seed of His Word in the soil of our lives, but the amount of harvest all depends on the condition of the heart. To be able to truly accept God's message ~ to believe it enough to act on it ~ our hearts must be humble and pure before the Lord. We must be willing to surrender our own ways, thoughts, and wills and want only His truth to grow, blossom, and bear fruit in our hearts and through our deeds. The more surrender the greater the crop!

Savor the Flavor...

Dear Lord, please tend the garden of my heart, till the hard places of unbelief, dig out the boulders of complacency, and remove the thorns of distraction that hinder my heart from the hundredfold!

Day 26

 Today's Apple...

But the fruit of the Spirit is love, joy, peace, patience, kindness, goodness, faithfulness, gentleness and self~control.

Galatians 5:22

Chew on it...

You are God's workmanship, and every day He is tending the fruit of His Spirit in your life. God's fruit, however, has not been natural to us since sin entered the Garden, and it often takes suffering and struggles for God's fruit to mature. You see, it's easy to love someone who loves you, but it takes God's love to love someone who has hurt you. It's one thing to have peace of mind when things are going well, but it's a God thing to have peace in the midst of the storm. It's easy to be patient when you see the answer, but it takes God's patience to wait for what you cannot see. You get the picture, I'm sure. God wants us to bear supernat~ural fruit ~ fruit that can only come as we allow His Spirit to rise up within us and flow through us to others.

Savor the Flavor...

Heavenly Father, help me to embrace Your grace in the struggles I face today. Show me where my fruit is shriveled or where I'm trying to develop my own fruit instead of yielding to You.

🍎 Today's Apple. . .

For they (God's words) are life to those who find them
and health to a man's whole body.

Proverbs 4:22

🍎 Chew on it. . .

Most of us are familiar with the age~old adage, "An apple a
day keeps the doctor away." Okay, so there's no guarantee
about the doctor, but the apple is known to improve one's
overall health significantly. God's Word is even better than
apples! Our minds and bodies are intricately linked together.
When our minds feed on God's truth and our thoughts chew on
what is good and wholesome and praiseworthy, it not only
brings health to our attitudes and emotions but also spills over
to affect the well~being of our whole body.

🍎 Savor the Flavor. . .

Heavenly Father, thank You for the banqueting table You have
spread before us as we look at the Bible as food for our souls.
Help me to clean out the mental junk food from my life and
eat only what pleases You.

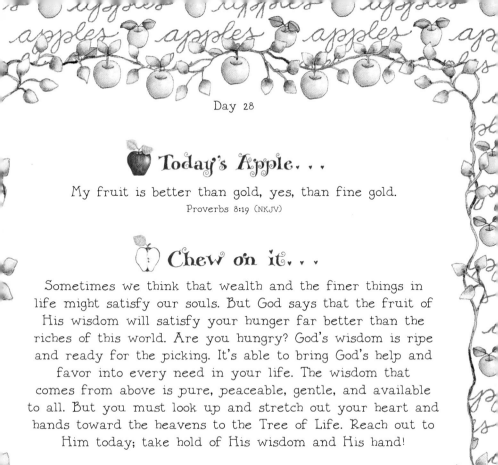

Day 28

🍎 Today's Apple...

My fruit is better than gold, yes, than fine gold.
Proverbs 8:19 (NKJV)

🍎 Chew on it...

Sometimes we think that wealth and the finer things in
life might satisfy our souls. But God says that the fruit of
His wisdom will satisfy your hunger far better than the
riches of this world. Are you hungry? God's wisdom is ripe
and ready for the picking. It's able to bring God's help and
favor into every need in your life. The wisdom that
comes from above is pure, peaceable, gentle, and available
to all. But you must look up and stretch out your heart and
hands toward the heavens to the Tree of Life. Reach out to
Him today; take hold of His wisdom and His hand!

🍎 Savor the Flavor...

Oh Lord, I confess I do not know how to handle my life on
my own. I need Your wisdom to show me what You want
me to do. Help me to listen expectantly for Your voice
and to not doubt Your power or desire to speak to my
heart and mind.

Apple Cake in a Jar

Preheat oven to 325 degrees.
Coat 8 pint~size, wide~mouth canning jars with cooking spray.
(Regular~mouth jars also work,
but cake will not come out in one piece.)

In a small bowl, mix together and set aside:

3 cups flour	1 tsp salt	2 tsp baking soda
½ tsp nutmeg	1 tsp cinnamon	½ tsp baking powder

In a large bowl, mix together:
⅔ cup shortening   2 ⅔ cups sugar   4 eggs

Add to the large bowl ⅔ cup of water and beat well. Slowly add
flour mixture from the small bowl, ½ cup at a time, and mix well.
Stir in 3 cups of peeled and grated apples.
(Try Granny Smith or Winesap.)
Stir in ⅔ cup raisins and ⅔ cup chopped nuts.
Fill each pre~sprayed wide~mouth jar with 1 cup of cake batter.
Bake on a cookie sheet on bottom rack for 45 minutes.
While jars are cooking, heat lids in a small amount of water on stove.
Remove from oven one jar at a time.
Seal each jar with hot lid and ring.

These are very fun gifts!

Cover the lid with a circle of fabric
the size of a salad plate and tie with a ribbon.
Use an attached tag to remind the recipient
that they are the apple of God's eye!

These will stay fresh in the jar
for up to three weeks!

Apple Trivia

Johnny Appleseed was born John Chapman in 1774.
Yes, he was a real person who earned his nickname
not only by scattering apple seeds hither and yon,
but by establishing several nurseries throughout Ohio and Indiana.
His efforts provided many pioneers with apple trees
and encouragement as they settled the Midwest.

According to legend, William Tell successfully shot an arrow
through an apple that was perched on the head of his young son.
I always thought he was foolishly showing off his skills,
but tradition says that it was his punishment for refusing
to salute a governor of his time.

Did an apple truly fall on Sir Isaac Newton's head?
It is believed to be true.
Amazing that a falling apple would be the foundation
of a theory that would change the universal understanding
of the laws of gravity!

On a hill stood a tree ~ a symbol of life and liberty

Today's Apple...

Walk as children of light (for the fruit of the Spirit
is in all goodness, righteousness, and truth),
finding out what is acceptable to the Lord.

Ephesians 5:8~10 (NKJV)

Chew on it...

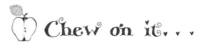

When we come to Christ, we are transplanted out of darkness
and into His glorious Light. The purity and power of His light
enable us, as His children, to bear the fruit of goodness,
righteousness, and truth in order to meet the challenges of daily
life. There will be seasons, though, when our circumstances,
attitudes, or wrong thinking will challenge us ~ hovering over our
heads and hearts like heavy clouds ~ and our fruitfulness will be
affected. But when we desire with all our hearts to please God
and bear healthy and holy fruit, He will show us not only what
is blocking His light, but how to move out from under it.

Savor the Flavor...

Father, let Your light shine brightly in my heart and reveal
any area of my life that is not pleasing to You ~ anything
that keeps me from bearing good fruit.

 **Today's Apple . . .**

When the king smiles, there is life;
his favor refreshes like a gentle rain.
Proverbs 16:15 (NLT)

Chew on it . . .

It's sad, but true . . . most Christians have never imagined that
King Jesus would smile at them. Have you? Why wouldn't He?
Don't those close to your heart make you smile? And don't you
sometimes smile at people you don't even know? Then why
wouldn't Jesus smile at you? You were made in the image of
God ~ you smile because He smiled first! Close your eyes for
just a moment and imagine Jesus smiling at you. The smile of His
favor will be like a refreshing rain upon your heart. And all of
us fruit~bearing trees need a gentle rain now and then,
don't you think?

Savor the Flavor . . .

Sweet Jesus, sometimes I get so busy trying to please You,
I confess I don't take the time to delight in You
like Your Word says You delight in me.
Thank You for the smile . . . and Your refreshing rain!

Imagine for a moment that you are sitting under an apple tree with Jesus. Close your eyes and look into His face. Can you see Him smiling at you? He is! He delights to be alone with you, even for a moment . . . this is a moment to savor!

Take another moment and write a prayer of thanksgiving to the Lord. Let Him know how much you delight in His smile.

Day 31

Today's Apple...

Taste and see that the LORD is good.
Psalm 34:8

Chew on it...

I was recently told a story about how every year the graduates of
a particular seminary would come together for their alumni picnic
and an opportunity to hear from a well~known theologian. That
year the speaker, a brilliant man, stood upon the platform and gave
a message that stunned the ears of all who listened as he denied
the claims and deity of Christ. All who were present sat stunned
and silent. Finally, in the crowd, an elderly man rose to his feet
holding a paper lunch bag in his hand. He reached into the bag,
pulled out an apple, and took a bite. He then addressed the speaker
by name, saying, "I'm not as eloquent a speaker as you or as
educated, but I have one question for you ~ is this apple bitter or
sweet?" The great theologian replied, "I don't know, I haven't tasted
it." To which, the elderly man responded, "Neither have you tasted
my Jesus" and sat down. You will know if you have tasted Him by
the flavor of His love that lingers in your heart.

Savor the Flavor...

Thank You, Lord, for the sweetness of Your love.

A Bushel Basket of Apple Facts

The smallest variety of apple is the crab apple. The flowers of the crab apple tree are gorgeous! (We just planted one in our yard!)

October is National Apple Month. That's the month to look for an apple festival in your area.

One of the very first jellybean flavors was apple. I wonder if it was a red, golden, or green variety.

The apple muffin is the official state muffin of New York! Do you think all states have an official muffin?

Moses Coates patented the apple parer in 1803. Thank you, Moses!

Over 80 percent of our country's apples are grown in only six states! The state of Washington, where I live, is one of those six.

Apples 5¢

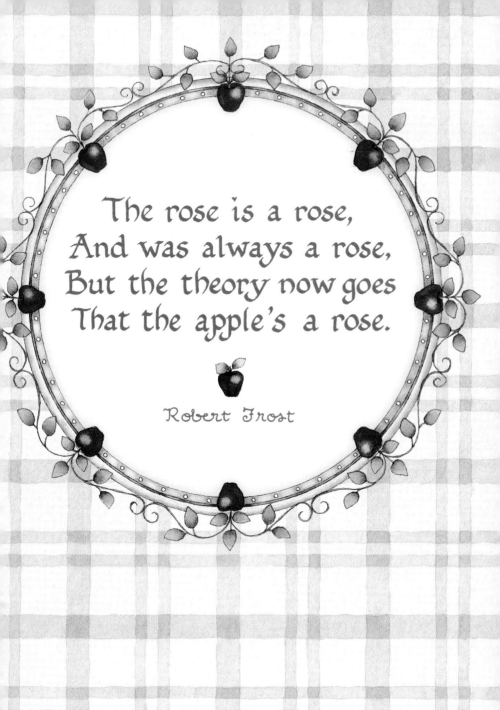

The rose is a rose,
And was always a rose,
But the theory now goes
That the apple's a rose.

Robert Frost

You thrill to God's Word,
you chew on Scripture
day and night.
You're a tree
replanted in Eden,
bearing fresh fruit
every month,
never dropping a leaf,
always in blossom.

Psalm 1:2~3 — The Message

Dear Friend,

God wants us to taste and see that He is good because
He is! And He wants us to grow, blossom, and bear
abundant fruit because then others can taste Him through
us. I know I want that, and I'm sure you do too!

I hope that as you've eaten your way through this
devotional and savored the sweetness of God's Word,
that your heart has been nourished and your branches
strengthened to bear abundant and mature fruit . . . fruit
that will nourish others and bless the heart of God!

And I pray that you will always be hungry . . .
hungry for an apple of God's Word every day to feed
your heart and satisfy your soul!

Thank you for allowing me to share my
heart with you once again in such a
delightful way!

For His glory
    and in His love,

        Karla

Other books from my heart and hand . . .

Savor This Moment

Life is short, isn't it? And our days are filled, sometimes to overflowing, with what seem to be just ordinary moments. But each moment we are given is a gift from God, and with the encouragement of this book your seemingly ordinary moments can become extraordinary as you discover God's presence and design in the midst of them. It's a great reminder to slow down and count blessings for all the busy women in your life, including you!

The Blessing of Friendship

Designed to celebrate the gift of friendship, both with Jesus and with other women, this book encourages us to look at the depth and the delights of embracing godly relationships. It includes several journaling pages, which make it an ideal gift to bless and encourage the women friends in your life.

Down a Garden Path

Stroll down the path of a very special garden and pause along the way to let God till the soil of your heart and plant a few seeds of faith. As you read, yield to a bit of divine pruning, or sit in the shade and simply enjoy the presence of the Lord. This gift book is not for your gardening friends only, but for any woman desiring to grow in her faith and walk with the Master Gardener of her soul. Great for new believers and seekers too.

Love in Every Room

Walk through a very special house where, room by room, you will be encouraged as a woman of God ~ and as the keeper of your home. Excellent gift for a housewarming party, bridal shower, or wedding, or just to encourage a woman's heart.

For more information on my books and gift products
or to share your thoughts and comments,
please write, email, or check out my website . . . I'd love to hear from you!

Karla Dornacher 🍎 1010 NE 104th Avenue 🍎 Vancouver, WA 98664
Karla@KarlaDornacher.com
www.KarlaDornacher.com